Small and Chic
HIGH STYLE FOR SMALL SPACES

Bridget Vranckx

Universe

First published in the United States of America in 2008
by UNIVERSE PUBLISHING
A Division of Rizzoli International Publications, Inc.
300 Park Avenue South
New York, NY 10010
www.rizzoliusa.com

Originally published in Spain in 2008 by
Loft Publications S.L.
Via Laietana 32, 4° Of. 92
08003 Barcelona, Spain
Tel.: +34 932 688 088
Fax: +34 932 687 073
loft@loftpublications.com
www.loftpublications.com

© 2008 Loft Publications S.L.
2008 2009 2010 2011 / 10 9 8 7 6 5 4 3 2 1

Printed in China

ISBN: 978-0-7893-1599-1

Library of Congress Control Number: 2007934234

Editor and text: Bridget Vranckx

Editorial Assistant: Esther Moreno

Managing Editor: Catherine Collin

Art Director: Mireia Casanovas Soley

Graphic design and Layout: Yolanda G. Román

Front cover photo © Christine Dempf
Back cover photo © Carlos Cezanne

Contents

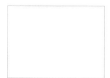

Introduction

According to the United Nations, the combined forces of population growth and urbanization will double the world's urban population by 2030 and more than half of the world's current 6.7 billion people will live in cities by 2008. As metropolitan communities increase, some cities are able to grow with them, while others have to reinvent themselves.

Many of the world's largest cities have seen a constant increase in population which has lead to a wider search for suitable living spaces and, ultimately, a reduction in the size of urban living. As well as the shortage of space, the unaffordable housing prices in major metropolises have called for a redefinition of urban homes. Now, more than ever, living in small spaces is becoming the norm rather than the exception and architects and interior designers are constantly finding new ways of making city living comfortable despite reduced dimensions.

Urbanites from New York to Shanghai and Hong Kong to Barcelona —be they young urban professionals or families—are willing to sacrifice space over location, but most will not compromise on comfort and style. Cosmopolites the world over are turning to original creations and innovative solutions to create their perfect luxurious havens in the city.

Because what is considered "small" is relative and varies from country to country, the projects presented in this book range from a tiny 300-square-foot apartment in New York to a 1,388-square-foot house in St. Kilda, Australia. Different types of dwellings, from new-builds to renovated spaces, are organized in three chapters: *tiny*, including interiors up to 646 square feet; *small*, urban pads ranging from 646 to 969 square feet; and *smallish*, dwellings up to 1,400 square feet.

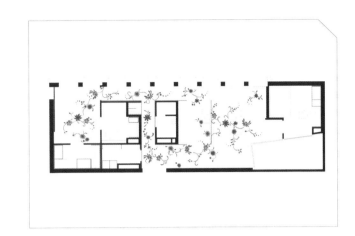

The following pages demonstrate that elegance and comfort need not be forsaken in condensed living environments thanks to thoughtful and efficient design, such as the use of color and innovative furniture and materials. Thus, a young Japanese family is able to live in a small, but unique, house in one of the world's largest cities, overcoming building restrictions and reduced plot sizes, and a New York resident can continue living in one of the world's most exclusive neighborhoods, albeit in a 300-square-foot rental property. Small-scale efficiency combined with opulence is also apparent in the 630-square-foot Hong Kong residence designed by PTang Studio and Greg Natale's sumptuous Sydney residence.

Tiny

Golden Handcuffs

Interior Designer: Robert Nassar

The tenant of this tiny apartment decided to finance a complete gut renovation, despite not being an owner, considering the importance of the property's exclusive location: New York City's Greenwich Village, one of the world's most desirable addresses. Living in a high-demand, high-priced neighborhood, the tenant chose to hold on to a small piece of affordable rental space, at any cost, rather than attempt to purchase the unaffordable.

With its high ceilings and two existing skylights, the volume of this diminutive apartment is visually expanded. The original wood floors were stained dark brown to further expand the space and eliminate inconsistent wood coloring. The apartment is divided into three rooms—living room, bedroom and bathroom—each one designed to reflect comfort, incorporate storage and exude style. A single wall-hung unit constructed of marine-grade plywood compresses dining, office, entertainment, library, and utility in one component. Similarly, the kitchen is built into a single niche. A stainless steel countertop creates a monolithic element and incorporates the sink and stop top, leaving plenty of prep counter space. Light-value, neutral colors, and limited furnishings and architectural details provide an overall sense of serenity throughout the apartment.

Surface: 300 sq ft

Location: New York, NY, USA

Completion date: 2004

Photos: © Rana Faure

Built-in cabinets with clean lines and flat panels provide floor-to-ceiling storage space. A niche on one side of the bed is the perfect place for some decorative details.

A recessed platform base makes the bed float weightlessly off the ground, visually reducing its mass. Limited furnishings and neutral colors exude a feeling of calm.

Tinted Box

Architect: OFIS Arhitekti

The brief for this 323-square-foot apartment in the cultural capital of Slovenia was to organize a comfortable urban home for a single male with a large living room. Because the living room had to be as large as possible, the additional required service spaces—entrance, kitchenette, workspace, bathroom, bedroom, and audio and video space—were reduced to an absolute minimum. The service areas create a kind of envelope around the main living space. These areas are separated from the living area by sliding doors made of semitransparent Perspex (polymethil metacrilate) with a blurry print. Each service area forms a sort of enclosed cupboard, which can be opened when needed and closed at other times. During the day, the envelope is totally opaque and like a solid wall when the doors are closed. At night, the boxes come alive as nocturnal lights are switched on in each individual box and the colors within bring out the blurry print on the Perspex doors.

Color is the main protagonist in this tiny apartment. It is painted white and is void of any decoration. The place comes alive with the light boxes that flood the room with atmospheric light and set the mood. Day and night, this small space is a luxurious haven in a city which exudes style and seems bigger than it is.

Surface: 323 sq ft

Location: Ljubljana, Slovenia

Completion date: 2004

Photos: © Tomaz Gregoric

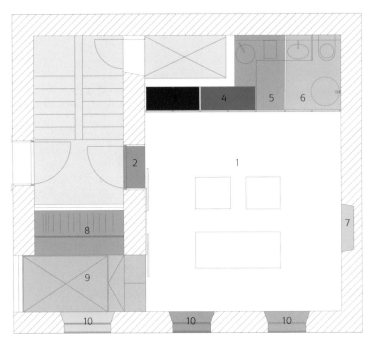

Floor plan

1. Living room
2. Entry box
3. Com box
4. TV box
5. Cook box
6. Toilet box
7. CD box
8. Wear box
9. Bed box
10. Light box

The sizes of the other elements in this tiny apartment are kept to a minimum so the living room can be as large as possible.

A blurry print on the semitransparent Perspex sliding doors is opaque during the day and comes alive at night when individual light boxes are switched on.

The service spaces including the bathroom, kitchenette, and audio and video space are placed around a large living area in boxed rooms which can be accessed when needed.

Rooftop Living

Architect: Queeste Architects

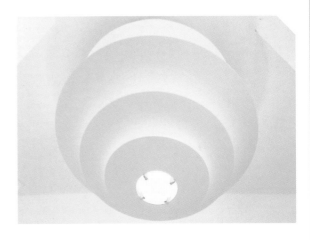

This apartment is situated on the third floor of a private house in The Hague, The Netherlands. Functioning autonomously from the rest of the building, the small apartment can be accessed via a communal staircase. The idea of this project was to create a comfortable living environment—despite the small volume—while providing all that is required for luxurious contemporary lodging. The small attic includes sleeping accommodations for two people, dining for four, a kitchen, toilet, bathroom with shower, and a number of storage facilities.

By using a very limited palette of forms and colors, the architects created a strong identity and sense of uniqueness. Rounded corners throughout imbue the small space with a sense of softness, while the overall use of white adds serenity to this multiformed space. The anthracite epoxy floors create a strong contrast with the white walls, ceiling, and furniture. The black and white color scheme is broken up by the warm orange pillows on the sofa. This color alludes to the predominantly orange rooftops of the city's historic center, visible from within this peaceful urban haven.

Surface: 323 sq ft

Location: The Hague, The Netherlands

Completion date: April 2007

Photos: © Teun van den Dries

The different areas of this small luxury lodging are grouped around one central open space. Rounded corners imbue this small space with a sense of softness.

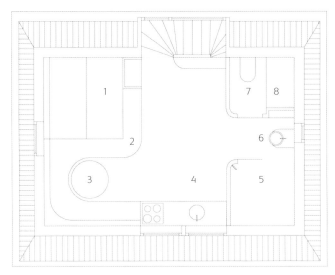

Floor plan

1. Bedroom
2. Living room
3. Dining room
4. Kitchen
5. Bathroom
6. Washbasin
7. Toilet
8. Installations room

The kitchen links the two areas of the apartment; the bathroom and storage room on one end and the bedroom and living room on the other.

Located at the rear (northeast) of the apartment, a
small garret window above the washbasin offers views
of a central courtyard.

Domestic Curio-Box

Architects: Gary Chang, Jerry She

A "domestic transformer," this project was an exercise in the extreme conditions of tight spaces; an experiment in fitting all the essential and unexpected activities of daily life into a compact 344.5-square-foot space without compromising anything. In order to create as complete a home as possible, an interactive 13 x 26 x 8-foot space with multifold capacities was created.

Considering the notions of change, choice, and connectivity, the architects designed components that play "hide-and-seek" with the inhabitants, a smart way of optimizing convenience and efficiency for compact living. One space easily transforms from a spacious living room to a kitchen; a small TV room to a bedroom. Similarly, a table can be pulled out when needed for work or dining necessities. The coldness of steel used throughout the small space is complemented by a warm glow of yellow light which filters through the shaded windows. The play of light on the shiny floor creates an interesting reflective effect, visually adding volume to this tiny space.

Surface: 344.5 sq ft

Location: Hong Kong, China

Completion date: 2007

Photos: © Edge Design Institute

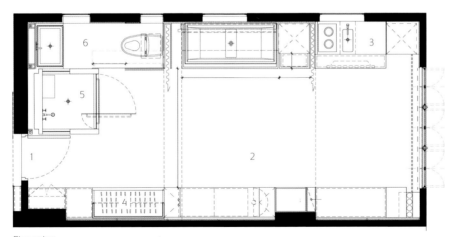

Floor plan

1. Entry
2. Living room
3. Kitchen
4. Closet
5. Shower
6. Bathroom

To optimize space and convenience, a table is pulled
out when needed and used for dining or working.

Opposites Attract

Architect: Silvestrin Salmaso Architects

Located in Berlin's fashionable district, Mitte, Lux 11 offers visitors a place to rest in style. Restored to its original glory, this former stately residential building now houses seventy-two impeccably designed apartments. The design concept developed by London-based architects Claudio Silvestrin and Giuliana Salmaso is inspired by the feeling of Berlin in recent years. Playing with the opposites found in Berlin interiors—mainly concrete and wood—the architects utilize the sensations of warmth and coolness, as well as smooth and rough textures in the design of this apartment.

A light minimalist color scheme—concrete in a subdued China green, brown leather curtains and upholstery, and warm wood—offers travelers a cool and modern ambience, with touches of tactile abundance and luxury. The hardness and roughness of the concrete is counteracted by gentle fabrics, such as the fluffy duvet and furlike pillows, giving the bed an opulent touch. Organized as an open space, the living area is separated from the bedroom by a central piece, while a strip of bamboo flooring links the bed with the sitting area and the desk at the other end of the room. Raised on a pedestal, a pristine bathroom unit sits almost altarlike in the middle and is separated from the main space by opaque glass. A dynamic use of space, proportion, and volume, combined with a purity of line and warm tones, creates a very powerful yet elegant environment.

Surface: 484 sq ft

Location: Berlin, Germany

Completion date: July 2005

Photos: © diephotodesigner.de

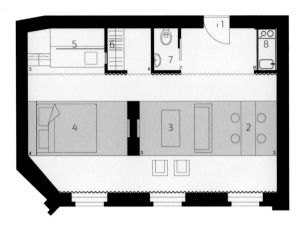

Floor plan

1. Entry
2. Study
3. Living room
4. Bedroom
5. Bathroom
6. Closet
7. Toilet
8. Kitchen

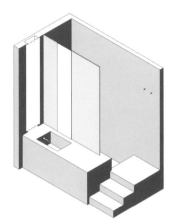

Axonometric bathroom

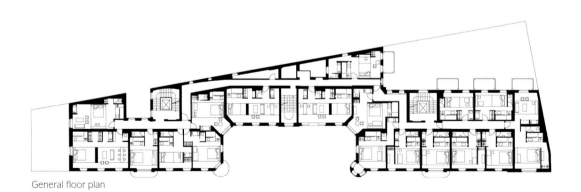

General floor plan

Reflecting modern Berlin interiors, the architects chose concrete and wood as the main materials of this luxury apartment in fashionable Berlin-Mitte.

A subtle and bespoke bathroom is part of the rest of the space. A light and minimalist color scheme creates a restful environment for the guest.

Top Views

Architect: Juan Antonio Gómez González

Making the most of its location at the top of *La Casa de les Lletres* (House of Letters), a collection of six themed apartments available for short- or long-term rental in Barcelona's hip El Born district, this bright attic combines an intelligent use of space with an aesthetic philosophy inspired by the Catalan poet, Joan Brossa.

A glass ceiling stamped with letters exposes the brilliant Mediterranean sky and creates continuity between the interior and exterior as well as closeness between the visitor and the Catalan writer. Comfort comes in the form of warm materials and vibrant colors. The "open" ceiling is a luxury in itself, enhanced by the deep brown wooden floorboards and brick walls which create a delightful and balanced contrast against the bright blue sky and white kitchen cabinets.

Surface: 484 sq ft

Location: Barcelona, Spain

Completion date: 2001

Photos: © Gogortza / Llorella

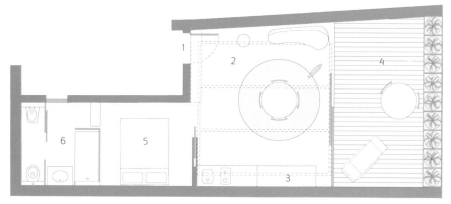

Floor plan

1. Entry
2. Living/dining room
3. Kitchen
4. Terrace
5. Bedroom
6. Bathroom

Clad in wood, a deluxe sleeping and bathing area is offset by exposed brick walls.

Separated by sliding wooden doors, the bedroom and bathroom make up a cozy privileged refuge off the main living and kitchen area.

Micro Miracle

Architect: CCS Architecture

This former studio apartment was transformed by creating a bedroom, abundant storage space, and a casual modern look, without adding square feet. A micro-bedroom with a queen-sized bed and storage below was inserted in what used to be a walk-in closet. Just for sleeping, this micro-bedroom has all the requisite bedside items such as a shelf and ledge for books, magazines, alarm clock, and reading light. Deep drawers under the bed from wall to entry provide maximum storage possibilities. The enclosure wall containing the bedroom is a partial-height, smooth, white wall with view ports through the living room and beyond. These rectangular view ports are positive visual elements throughout the rest of the apartment.

The main space, which was originally used as a bedroom and living room, is now furnished for eating or working at a central table; living and relaxing at a central sofa; and storage and display with full-height wall cabinets. The all-white room is adorned with selective mirrors to maximize spaciousness and visual simplicity. Overall, the architect has managed to create an extremely functional and stylish one-bedroom apartment in a limited space.

Surface: 500 sq ft

Location: New York, NY, USA

Completion date: January 2006

Photos: © Javier Haddad Conde

Original floor plan

1. Entry
2. Bedroom
3. Closet
4. Bathroom
5. Kitchen

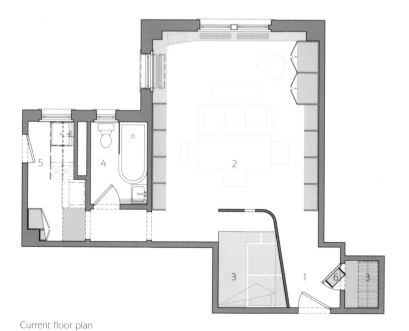

New storage areas

	Full height
	Below
	Above

1. Entry
2. Living room
3. Bedrooms
4. Bathroom
5. Kitchen
6. Closet

Current floor plan

What used to be a closet has been transformed into a sleeping alcove accommodating a queen-sized bed with plenty of storage below.

Just big enough to fit a bed, this micro-bedroom has all the requisite bedside items, including a shelf and ledge for books, alarm clock, and reading light.

Bittersweet Symmetry

Architect: Cássio & Associados

The main aim of the architects of this small apartment in Oporto was to de-clutter and create a bright and luminous home on a small budget. The single young male living here needed extra storage space and bookshelves for his extensive collection of books and publications, as well as space for a small work area. Sticking to simple modern lines and plain colors, the architects created a modern home which seems bigger than it is.

Despite the limited square-footage of this apartment, the architects managed to create multiple spaces—an area for living, working, sleeping, bathing, and cooking—without compromising space. By applying varied yet plain colors, different domestic areas were defined, while sticking to furniture with simple modern lines and clear colors helped create the illusion of a bigger space. Thus, a burgundy wall characterizes the home's main living area and a simple black bookshelf and clear-colored rectangular desk in one corner of this room comprise the study area. As well as creating a clear distinction of spaces, the choice of burgundy for one of the walls and one of the sofas in the living space adds a touch of sophistication to this room.

Surface: 538 sq ft

Location: Oporto, Portugal

Completion date: January 2005

Photos: © Carlos Cezanne

The choice of furniture with simple modern lines and
in clean colors creates the illusion of a bigger space.

Divine Abode

Architect: Jonathan Clark Architects

Situated at the top of a converted church in Westbourne Grove—in London's Notting Hill—this newly built shell space was converted into an elegant penthouse apartment. The unit was designed as an open plan space with a sleeping area that could be separated from the main living area with light diffusing panels. Floating ceiling rafts and raised coffers with recessed lighting were designed especially to give a greater sense of height and volume, as well as providing a sense of drama to the space. No detail has been overlooked in this deluxe apartment: electronic wrap-around curtains give an extra degree of privacy at night; an integrated AV system with ceiling-mounted speakers help create a seamless look; and comfort cooling and a high degree of glazing has been installed for ultimate luxury living.

The floor-to-ceiling windows in the living and sleeping area provide interesting views over the emblematic rooftops of the surrounding terraced houses in this trendy London neighborhood. These are reflected in the kitchen's mirrored splash back, thus increasing the feeling of space as well as providing a view while cooking.

Surface: 549 sq ft

Location: London, United Kingdom

Completion date: July 2005

Photos: © Jonathan Clark

A new 549-square-foot shell space on top of a converted church was transformed into a luxury penthouse apartment in the heart of London's Notting Hill.

To counter the low 8.5 foot ceiling height, floating ceiling rafts and raised coffers with recessed lighting were installed to create a sense of volume and height.

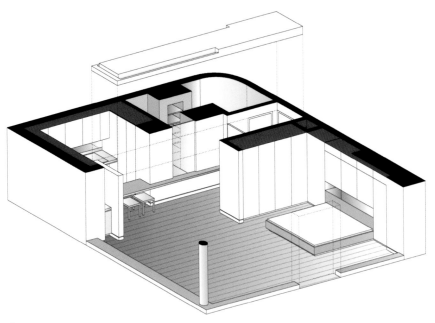

Axonometry

Floor plan

1. Entry
2. Bathroom
3. Kitchen
4. Living room
5. Bedroom

The sleeping area can be sectioned off from the main living area and an integrated AV system with ceiling mounted speakers helps create a seamless look.

Historic Luxury

Architect: Judith Farran

This small luxury tourist apartment in the historic center of Barcelona in a renovated building is clearly divided into day and night areas. One large room incorporates the day areas—entrance hall, living room, and dining area—on one side, while the bedroom and bathroom are on the other. Incorporating the original structures of the old building adds character to this small urban home.

By concentrating several domestic tasks in one open space and using neutral colors and transparent materials, the architects managed to create an apartment that feels much bigger than it is. Despite its small dimensions, it can comfortably house four people, thanks to a sofa bed in the living room. A double wall was created in the adjacent master bedroom to make room for a closet. A backlit white structure which stretches the length of the wall behind the bed makes for a smart wardrobe. A shelf is cut out of the structure for bedside items, such as a night lamp. Making the most of every last inch without compromising luxury and comfort, the small desk in the bedroom can be used as a dressing table or working area.

Surface: 592 sq ft

Location: Barcelona, Spain

Completion date: 2002

Photos: © Gogortza / Llorella

The use of neutral colors, transparent materials, and straight lines in the furniture helps create an illusion of space.

This small urban apartment is divided into two main spaces: the day areas on one side and the night area on the other.

The original structures of this building in the historic
center of Barcelona are incorporated into the design of
this luxury apartment.

A white backlit structure behind the bed in the master
bedroom provides space for a walk-in closet—a luxury
often reserved for larger residences.

Every last inch is used without cluttering the
space too much. Soft neutral colors and lighting
create a relaxed environment.

Rethinking the Tenement

Architect: Ghiora Aharoni Design Studio

Situated in a 1903 tenement building originally built to house Italian-American families of Greenwich Village, this small Manhattan apartment has had a remarkable twenty-first century facelift, without compromising its past. Considering its landmark status and protective regulations, the sensitive renovation of this home included the revelation of brick walls, ceiling beams, and wooden studs hidden beneath layers of paint and plaster. Original walls were knocked down and the entire interior was demolished, conserving the memory of the apartment's original floor plan, which is visible in the configuration of the ceiling beams.

An eclectic collection of art and furniture gracefully blends with custom-designed items, innovative features, and space-enhancing elements, in perfect harmony with the space's historical past. Oversized mirrors visually enlarge the living and dining area and showcase the antique schoolhouse chairs around the dining table and a wide solar shade descends from the ceiling to section off the open kitchen and provide a projection surface for film screenings. The architect designed cabinets and bookshelves in the kitchen to float above a newly installed floor of wide-board American cherry, thus creating sleek and clutter-free storage space.

Surface: 600 sq ft

Location: New York, NY, USA

Completion date: 2004

Photos: © Floto + Warner

The furniture in this Greenwich Village apartment
ranges from midcentury classics like the chair and
ottoman by Paul Lázló to antique schoolhouse chairs
around the dining table.

Oversized mirrors enhance the space and put some of
the owner's eclectic art collection and furniture on
display; for example, the Ellsworth Kelly paintings and
Asian sculptures.

Rendering

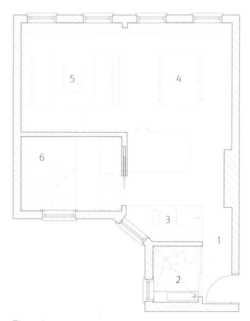

Floor plan

1. Entrance
2. Bathroom
3. Kitchen
4. Dining room
5. Living room
6. Bedroom

Oriental Style

Architect: PTang Studio Limited

The dividing walls of this former two-bedroom apartment were knocked down to create the ultimate deluxe urban pad in Hong Kong's Sham Tseng area, famous for its spectacular views of the Tsing Ma Bridge over the Ma Wan Channel. Combining white walls and tiles with transparent and almost futuristic pieces of furniture and reflective materials, Philip Tang and Brian Ip of PTang Studio created a splendid residential interior.

First of all, the original two bedrooms were combined to create one master bedroom. A bespoke gold-tinted glass cabinet with a large plasma screen TV visually separates the night area from the main living area. At the same time, this piece of furniture also allows the two spaces to interact when the cabinet is rotated so the denizens can watch their favorite shows from either the living room or the bedroom. The night zone is clearly differentiated from the rest of the space by its darker tones. Other design "tricks" such as the use of white walls and tiles throughout help make the 630-square-foot-space seem bigger. Philippe Starck's elegant glass Louis Ghost chairs reflected in a wonderfully large mirror in the dining room not only add a sense of transparency and spaciousness, but a touch of elegance as well.

Surface: 630 sq ft

Location: Hong Kong, China

Completion date: January 2006

Photos: © Ulso Tang

Floor plan

1. Entrance
2. Dining room
3. Kitchen
4. Living room
5. Revolving cabinet
6. Bedroom
7. Bathroom
8. Balcony

White walls and tiles, and the use of reflective and transparent materials such as glass and plastic, create a futuristic "cyber" effect.

The bedroom is differentiated from the living and
dining area by its dark tones and subtle lighting.

A rotating glass cabinet with a large plasma screen TV
separates the bedroom from the living room and can
be rotated according to the occupant's desires.

A bespoke desk in the night area makes perfect use of
limited space.

Capital Delight

Architect: Pablo Paniagua

Situated in a late eighteenth-century building in Madrid's historic center, this apartment was an old storage room on the roof before Pablo Paniagua turned it into a small luxury urban apartment. Making the most of the openness of the space, the architect tried to bring together domestic functions with as little physical compartmentalization as possible.

The entrance to the apartment functions as a reception hall, kitchen, and dining area, at the same time, while the home's main space is the living room—a place for gathering around the chimney and working in the library against the wall. The bedroom sits off this main space and can be separated from the living and working area by sliding doors. The aesthetic choice of materials and decoration makes for a timeless and neutral, yet strong, interior design. Ash-colored oak floorboards and limestone walls create the perfect backdrop for an exquisite repertoire of decorative elements ranging from eighteen to twenty-first-century pieces, complemented by the gleaming black lacquer and brown matte finishes of the kitchen and library, the sandstone chimney, and white-lacquered carpentry.

Surface: 630 sq ft

Location: Madrid, Spain

Completion date: 2007

Photos: © Pablo Paniagua

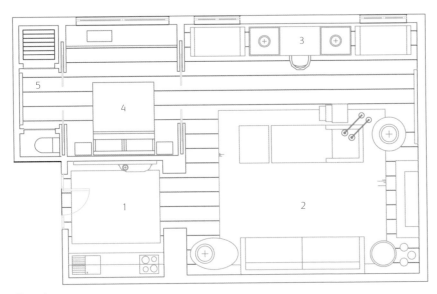

Floor plan

1. Entrance/kitchen/dining room
2. Living room
3. Study
4. Bedroom
5. Bathroom

Small

Bold Times

Architect: Target Living

Renowned for their bold style, strong use of color, and understanding of space, Tara Bernerd and her partner Thomas Griem were called upon to design an exciting studio apartment in London's elite development "The Knightsbridge." The brief was to introduce a more contemporary feel. Specializing in functioning and desirable environments with a touch of genuine value, the design duo focused on the potential demands of such a small space, while paying attention to detail and a way of life.

Clearly separating the domestic areas in this limited space was fundamental, so the designers created different zones for sleeping, eating, and relaxing. One of the key features of this urban pad is a raised white lacquer platform for the bed area. By raising it slightly off the ground, this zone is distinguished from the other areas. A moody tinted mirror and retro leather seating define the dining area while white screen fringe curtains separate the sleeping area from the rest of the space. The hallway into the bathroom is utilized as a work area and given a unique personality with flowery wallpaper. The combination of a rich palette of charcoal gray and bright orange colors with a mix of indulgent materials creates a unique urban studio apartment.

Surface: 645 sq ft

Location: London, United Kingdom

Completion date: September 2005

Photos: © Philip Vile

A mix of bright colors and rich materials helps define
the different domestic areas in this small apartment.

A raised white lacquer platform sets the bedroom
apart from the rest of this small studio apartment.

White fringe curtains create a separating screen
between the night zone and relaxation area,
without blocking them off completely.

The room leading to the bathroom is used as a
study/library and given unique character with
flowered wallpaper.

Origami House

Architect: García & Ruiz Architecture Design

First presented at Casa Décor Barcelona 2006 for the electrical appliances firm Whirlpool, Origami House was designed to make the most of limited available space. To optimize square footage and give it a sense of movement, the architects created a triangular-shaped structure of white-painted wood, which contains the domestic areas and folds like a piece of origami paper. Each domestic space opens out onto the fold's center of inertia, thus creating more room and allowing each area—living, dining, cooking, storing, cleaning, and sleeping—to develop its own function identity around this center.

The three-dimensional and slightly futuristic look, created by the myriad of diagonals in movement and the predominance of white, is complemented by ultramodern technological features and sophisticated electrical appliances worthy of mention, such as Whirlpool's In.home (a project that explores the way a home can change and adapt according to the changing patterns of behavior and moods of the people living there), the innovative column for washing and drying clothes in the laundry area and the built-in refrigerator and dishwasher, which look like any other drawer in the kitchen. Without a doubt, this is a twenty-first-century home that does not compromise on luxury, comfort, originality, or innovation.

Surface: 646 sq ft

Location: Barcelona, Spain

Completion date: 2006

Photos: © Pedro M. Mahamud

The wooden structure bends and defines movement throughout the home. The common areas open out onto the entrance, while the more private spaces are hidden out of sight.

The wooden frame is painted a luminous white with ultraresistant paint by Valentine, which gives this interior a stylish futuristic look. The sofa made of rolls is designed by García & Ruiz Design.

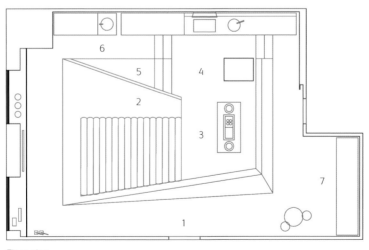

Floor plan

1. Entry
2. Sofa
3. Dining room
4. Kitchen
5. Stairs
6. Bathroom
7. Laundry room

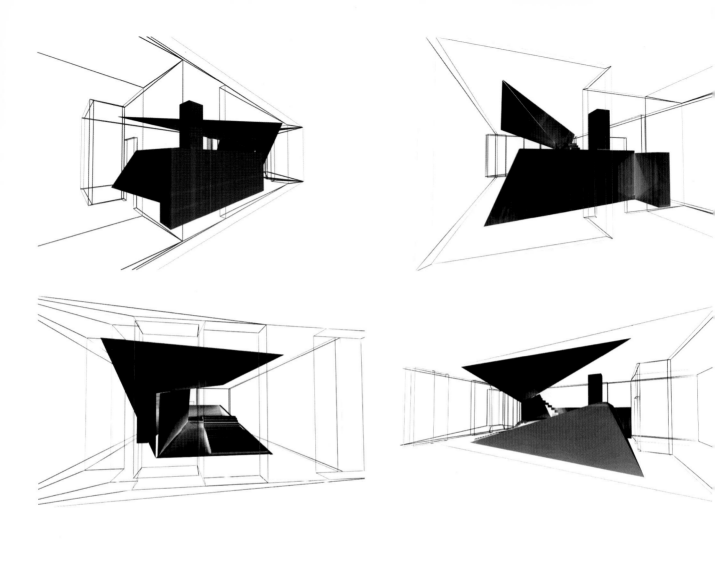

The dining area, made up of a white table and chairs by Sit Down, connects the living space and high-tech kitchen with electrical appliances by Whirlpool.

The lighting adds a special touch to the already unique interior design of this urban home; spotlights placed throughout the home create a particular ambience for each space.

The communal areas open out onto a center of inertia, while more private spaces, such as the sleeping and bathing areas, are tucked away behind the folds of the structure.

The most private space is reserved for the bedroom
upstairs. A small corner tucked away beneath the
stairs is used as a dressing table, decorated with vases
by Habitat.

To maintain an overall sleek look, certain kitchen
appliances, such as the dishwasher and refrigerator,
are hidden inside what seem to be drawers.

Poised Elegance

Architect: García & Ruiz Architecture Design

Once a dark apartment with a claustrophobic windowless hallway, this 646-square-foot apartment with a 538-square-foot terrace is now the bright and open urban home of architect Héctor Ruiz Velázquez, where he lives with his wife and son. In order to let in plenty of light and make the most of every last centimeter, Héctor and Javier Garcia Garcia turned to basic theatre tricks such as forced perspectives to achieve much wider spatial perceptions. Color and illumination are other design tricks used throughout: white creates the illusion of spaciousness and black dots and vertical surfaces in certain areas create the feeling of extra depth.

The hallway was the starting point of this project and is the apartment's most impressive feature. A dynamic axis emerging from the entrance makes its way down to the main living area—guided by round black IKEA carpets—leaving static spaces on either side of the three-dimensional diagonal. Doors without handles open out onto a bed-room, bathroom, and guest room-cum-study. The movement of the curvilinear hallway culminates in the aerodynamic kitchen and dining area, which opens out onto the terrace that has been turned into a living room. The rooms at the end of the corridor are further defined by differences in height, to accentuate the contrasts even further.

Surface: 646 sq ft

Location: Madrid, Spain

Completion date: December 2006

Photos: © Belén Imaz

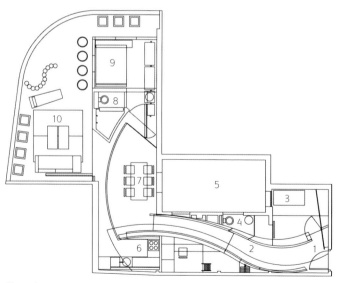

Floor plan

1. Entry
2. Curved hallway
3. Bedroom
4. Bathroom
5. Guest room/office
6. Kitchen
7. Dining room
8. Master bedroom
9. Master bathroom
10. Living room/terrace

The bedroom is surrounded by huge floor-to-ceiling
windows which open out onto the large terrace,
making the room bright and airy.

A large steel and glass door separates the bedroom
from the living area. A light transparent ceiling gives
the impression one is sleeping in the open air.

The use of glass, the color white, and suspended
sanitary elements give the bathroom depth and
a quality of light.

Front-to-Back House

Architect: Scape Architects

A compact mews house in the heart of London's bustling Islington neighborhood is not only a sacrifice of space over location for the city dweller, but also a creative challenge for the architect. With a total floor space of 650 square feet, space is tight and design ingenuity and craftsmanship a must. Working closely with the director of Scape Architects, Chris Godfrey, the owners have a tailor-made home which suits their needs and that of the site.

The property is enclosed on all three sides by adjacent buildings and a schoolyard. New windows were arranged on the facade to let more daylight in: translucent glazing was installed on the ground floor and opaque fabric screens on the upper level to ensure privacy from the road. Inside, the house is lit from a skylight above and artificial lighting. The stair is the hub of the house and provides the principal light source, day and night, to the entire house. The bespoke staircase, clearly defined from the rest of the interiors by a diamond patterned black tread, runs to the apex of the house and divides the bedroom from the bathroom on the first level and the kitchen from the front entrance below. Moreover, at ground level, the structure provides dual-sided storage without compromising the overall look of the interior. It houses bicycles, coats, and integrated AV system on the living side and kitchenware and a guest bathroom on the other.

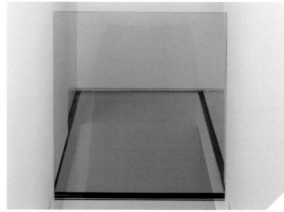

Surface: 646 sq ft

Location: London, United Kingdom

Completion date: april 2007

Photos: © Michele Panzeri

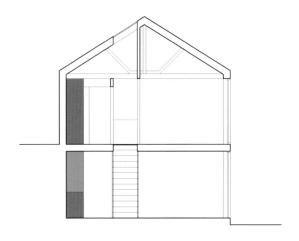

Sections

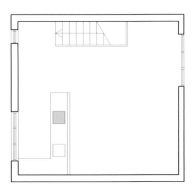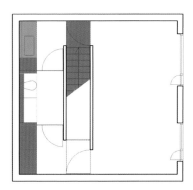

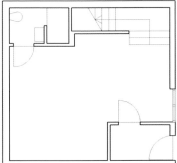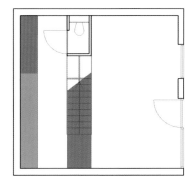

Floor plans

Translucent glazing on the ground level of a compact
mews house ensures privacy without blocking daylight.

The palette of materials is minimized and used
to accentuate spatial concepts and highlight
sculptural form.

A glass platform opposite the apex of the stair filters daylight down from the skylight above to the rest of the house and links the upstairs rooms.

White walls, limited furniture, and a soft color scheme create the perfect relaxed environment for a good night's rest.

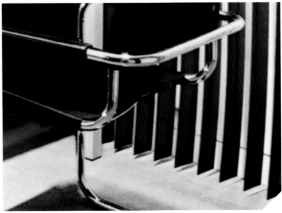

Small Feat

Architect: Ajax Law Ling Kit, Virginia Lung

Even though interior designers in Hong Kong are used to working with small spaces, this apartment was the most challenging project yet for these designers. The brief called for the three basic functions—working, entertaining, and relaxing—to be accommodated in a 650-square-foot space and for the mood of the apartment to be changeable to suit the event.

With their changeable wallpaper, the designers of this small apartment created an interactive space with exciting dimensions of imaginary spaces. Interconnected modules, movable furniture, and blurred boundaries provide a dynamic spatial relationship. The use of vertical blinds and sliding doors allows for different multiple interior atmospheres to be created according to the needs of the event. One side of the blind has a mirror finish and, the other, a glossy red paint finish. Reflective materials not only double the volume of a space, but fragments of mirrors also create illusions of what is real and unreal. Add to this the flashing disco light and the stimulating red color to create the perfect party ambience. The positive and active aspect of the color red is also perfect for the work environment. For day-to-day use, the blinds can be opened to expose the gray walls and create a calm and soothing atmosphere. In short, this Hong Kong residence is a highly flexible small space which maximizes both space and mood.

Surface: 646 sq ft

Location: Hong Kong, China

Completion date: december 2004

Photos: © Ajax Law Ling Kit, Virginia Lung

party

living

task

recharge

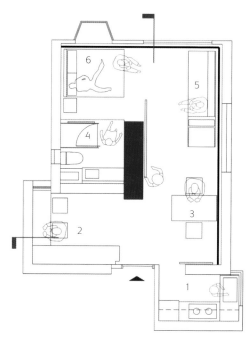

Floor plan

1. Kitchen
2. Study
3. Reading area
4. Bathroom
5. Living room
6. Bedroom

To create a place of freedom without boundaries, the blinds can be turned to reveal fragments of mirrors and generate illusions of what is real and unreal.

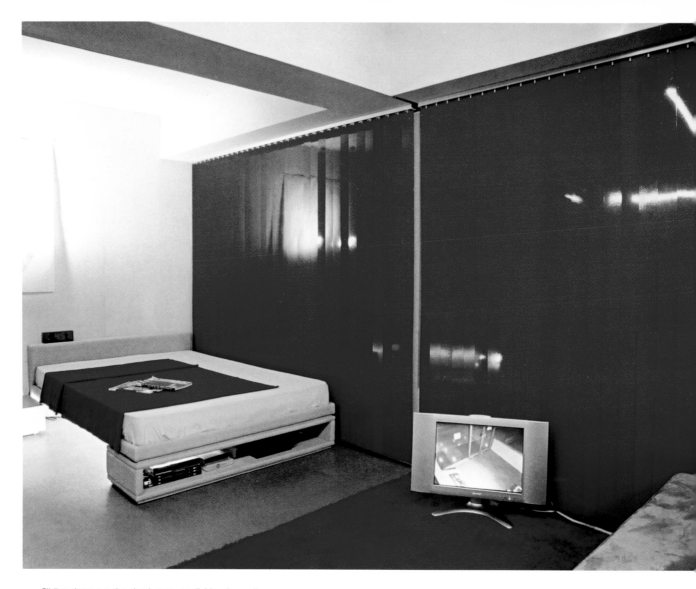

Sliding doors are the absolute space dividers in small spaces. Here the bedroom can be separated from the rest of the space or integrated, and the mood changes accordingly at a flick of the blinds.

Singular Charm

Architect: Cornelie Tollens

This urban home in the Dutch capital is situated in an original 1649 building, which was subdivided into apartments in 1994. Designed by the owner himself and executed by a timber specialist, this small double-height urban home is full of quirky details, both added by the owner and retained from the original structure.

The high ceiling gives the place more volume and sensation of space. Making the most of this height, a mezzanine was created to house a bedroom, leaving space for the bathroom, toilet, and living room below. The bedroom forms a cozy attic space which can be closed off with curtains to create more privacy. The Art Nouveau ornaments on the ceiling and the fireplace are original elements that Cornelie decided to maintain and incorporate into the design of his urban home, complementing them with an eclectic collection of furniture and antiques and bringing the whole together with a limited color scheme of brown, black, and red tones.

Surface: 646 sq ft

Location: Amsterdam, The Netherlands

Completion date: January 2006

Photos: © Carlos Cezanne / Attitude

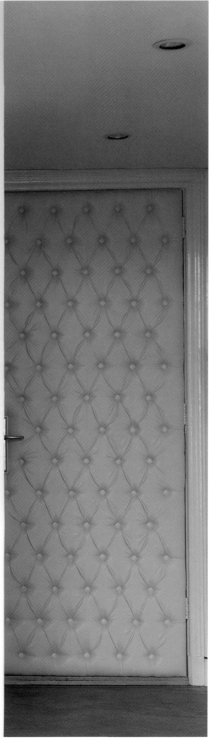

Despite the eclectic mix of modern and antique furniture, the use of particular colors throughout gives this small apartment in Amsterdam a unique old-time elegance.

A small apartment does not mean solid furniture cannot be used. In this case, the living room is big enough to create a living and work area with an old-fashioned desk.

Complementing a classic kitchen unit with elements
not normally associated with this part of the house,
such as a night lamp and a classic painting, creates
interesting ambience.

Romantic Modernism

Architect: Juan Antonio Gómez González

Another apartment in Barcelona's La Casa de les Lletres, this three-bedroom apartment pays homage to the Catalan author Mercè Rodoreda and the special typology of Catalan Modernism. Original architectural structures, such as the walls and floor tiles, are enhanced with modern-day lighting to create an inviting environment.

Working with a rectangular floor plan, the architects created a spacious apartment that includes a living and dining area, large kitchen, and bathroom in only 645 square feet. By placing the three bedrooms next to each other, the space naturally opens itself to create a comfortable living and dining room. Applying warm colors to the plastered bedroom walls creates cozy rooms and reflects the elegance of the original exposed brickwork and floor tiles.

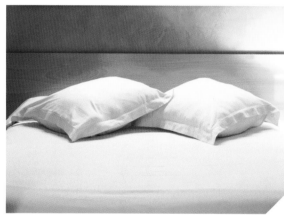

Surface: 646 sq ft

Location: Barcelona, Spain

Completion date: 2001

Photos: © Gogortza / Llorella

"I vaig pujar al terrat a respirar. Em vaig
acostar a la baranda de la banda del carrer
i em vaig quedar quieta allà una estona.
Feia vent."

Mercè Rodoreda
La plaça
1962

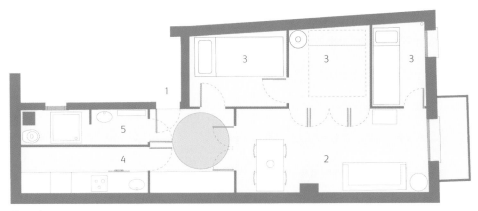

Floor plan

1. Entry
2. Living/dining room
3. Bedroom
4. Kitchen
5. Bathroom

Warm materials and colors are used to create a cozy
ambience and also to pay homage to the original
architectural elements of Catalan Modernism.

The writer's prose and thoughts fill the rooms of this
short-term rental apartment and give the visitor a
unique taste of Barcelona.

Twisted Logic

Architect: Akira Yoneda, Masahiro Ikeda

Situated in a favorable location within the Tokyo metropolitan area, the site is rather modest. However, Akira Yoneda (Architecton) and Masahiro Ikeda turned the 539-square-foot space into a small family home with 664 square feet of living space, using only 323 square feet for construction. Besides the limited square footage, the architects were also faced with the problems of ensuring parking space and plenty of natural light. The site opens out on the north side onto the street and is closely packed on the other sides by neighboring houses, making the possibility of natural light extremely difficult.

A rectangular shape ensured optimal building coverage and defined the building's outline on the above-ground level by diagonal lines that avert the parking space. A skylight in the roof ensured that the whole interior of the building is illuminated from above. Connecting the lines along the roof surface and the oblique lines on the above-ground level, parallel lines gradually twisted and developed into hyperbolic-paraboloids, which shape the building's exterior walls. Moreover, the indoor convex surfaces and outdoor concave surfaces provide externality to internal spaces and internality to external spaces, thus creating a reversed indoor/outdoor effect. A volume housing the children's room on the third floor includes a tubelike shape and a double-height void and is painted a metallic orange, which allows reflections of color and spatial images in addition to reflections of light from the skylight.

Surface: 667 sq ft

Location: Tokyo, Japan

Completion date: May 2004

Photos: © Koji Okumura

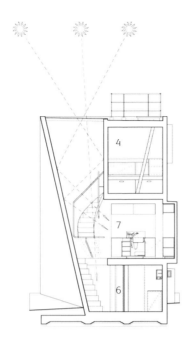

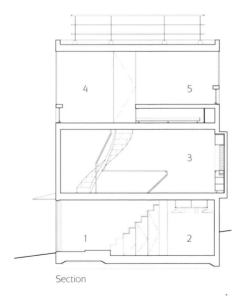

Section

1. Entry
2. Closet
3. Living/dining room
4. Living room
5. Bedroom
6. Storage
7. Kitchen

A skylight in the roof ensures that this three-story
north-facing house in a dense urban area enjoys
plenty of natural light.

With a sweeping gesture, a hyperbolic-paraboloid
surface performs sculpturally, functionally,
and structurally.

In response to the reflection of light, a volume housing the children's room on the third floor is painted metallic orange to catch reflections of color and spatial images.

Latin Legacy

Architect: Greg Natale

This project is the architect's own personal space. He wanted to create an original home reflecting himself and his experiences. The design hones in on three different looks: the owner's Italian-Australian background, the decade in which he was born—the 1970s—and contemporary design. A baroque chair from his family home, a Murano pendant light, a baroque headboard and Basalt floors are a tribute to the architect's Italian heritage. To create drama and contrast from the rest of the white building, the apartment was painted charcoal gray. Mirrors turn the kitchen into a wet bar, while a high gloss ebony credenza, fur rug, and stucco wall add glamour. The taffeta curtains create a theatrical look and the restored 1970s dining chairs in rich brown velvet add a touch of sophistication.

The apartment's straight lines are the perfect backdrop to the chosen decoration. The gray walls are complementary to the rich brown tones of the upholstery and joinery and also bring out the pinks in the Warhol and Murano chandelier. The dark gray also helps soften the minimalist shell of the apartment while at the same time strengthening the straight lines. The overall effect of the warm tone is moody, cocooning, and opulent.

Surface: 753 sq ft

Location: Sydney, Australia

Completion date: December 2005

Photos: © Sharrin Rees

The apartment's straight lines contrast and play
together nicely with the chosen decoration.

The use of reflective materials in the kitchen helps create depth and gives this area a sleek, polished, and unique look.

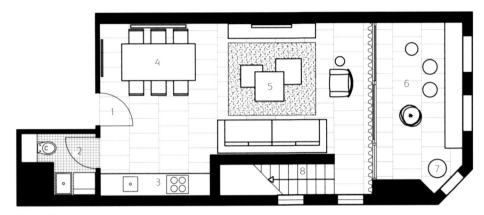

Ground floor

1. Entry
2. Laundry room
3. Kitchen
4. Dining room
5. Living room
6. Terrace
7. Barbecue
8. Stairs

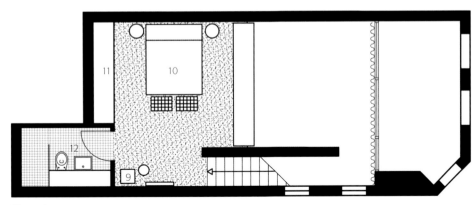

Mezzanine

Floor plans

9. Dressing room
10. Bedroom
11. Closet
12. Bathroom

The gray walls complement the rich brown tones and add a touch of warmth.

A baroque headboard pays homage to the owner's Italian heritage and also creates an opulent ambience.

Executive Repose

Architect: Ajax Law Ling Kit, Virginia Lung

The Gateway is a business apartment development in Shenzhen which caters to businessmen's increasing demand for comfortable temporary residences. Conveniently located between Hong Kong and Shenzhen to suit the needs of Hong Kong residents who frequently commute to Shenzhen for work purposes, The Gateway offers a variety of apartments ranging in size from 387 to 775 square feet. These units offer a creative and comfortable alternative to the dull standardized hotel room. Each has its unique characteristics and reflects the profiles and needs of the businessman who occupy them.

The Entrepreneur is the largest suite created by this Hong Kong company hoping to steer the design of apartment hotels in a new direction. To reflect the characteristic high-class lifestyle of entrepreneurs, the designers chose hues of gold and dark and light brown colors. The use of these colors synonymous with luxury is combined with materials akin to opulence such as the dark marble used in the kitchen and bathroom. To create the feeling of space, reflective materials such as mirrors are widely used. Thus, the deluxe bedroom and en suite bathroom are enlarged by inserting mirrors, while yellow glass adds a glamorous touch.

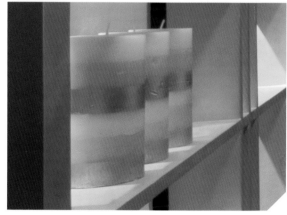

Surface: 775 sq ft

Location: Shenzhen, China

Completion date: 2006

Photos: © Gabriel Leung

Floor plan

1. Kitchen
2. Dining room
3. Living room
4. Balcony
5. Master bedroom
6. Master bathroom
7. Study
8. Bathroom
9. Guest room

To create an apartment characteristic of
an entrepreneur's lifestyle, the designers chose
luxurious colors and materials, such as shades
of gold and brown and marble and velvet.

Mirrors are used in the master bedroom and
bathroom to enhance the space and extend
its elegance.

Metropolitan Chic

Architect: Mohen Design International

Challenged to design a small residential interior in a Shanghai apartment building, the designers sought a careful balance and way of providing sufficient storage without compromising either aesthetics or space. The areas of this compact two-bedroom apartment are clearly separated; the hallway splits the space in two, situating the kitchen and master bedroom opposite the living area and guest room/study. Decoration has been left to a minimum, concentrating instead on the spacious visual effects of line, uneven surfaces, and ceiling lighting to further delimit spaces. The generous use of mirrors in the entrance, kitchen, and master bedroom, for example, also helps make this small living space seem bigger, while the use of light yellow and brown colors and dimmed lighting give the place a simple yet elegant look, accentuating the contrast of the clear lines of the glass surfaces at the same time.

The importance of hidden storage is greater in small spaces where too many objects on view can easily make a place look small and cluttered. The mirrored cupboard in the hallway neatly hides shoes, umbrellas, and keys. The uneven living room wall cleverly conceals a large CD collection. Similarly, rooms can have double functions. Thus, the bespoke sofa bed in the guest room/study can be used as a comfortable reading area when not used for guests.

Surface: 796 sq ft

Location: Shanghai, China

Completion date: 2006

Photos: © Mohen Design International

Light colors and smooth surfaces combined with subtle lighting create a warm, contemporary, and refined interior.

A large mirrored cupboard in the hallway effectively hides footwear and other items, while the living room wall cunningly conceals a collection of CDs.

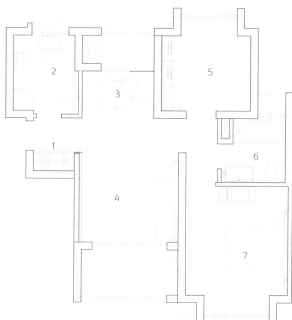

Floor plan

1. Entry
2. Kitchen
3. Dining room
4. Living room
5. Master bedroom
6. Bathroom
7. Guest room/study

The owner of this apartment can be ready for any situation with a specially designed sofa bed in the guest room/study, which can also be used as a private space.

On Show

Architect: New ID Interiors

In view of the price of housing in big cities, property buyers and developers alike are moving to the outskirts of metropolises for quality and fashionable urban living spaces at affordable prices. Thus, a prestigious complex by Irish developers Gannon Homes contains seven one-bedroom and seven two-bedroom apartments in East Dulwich, just outside Central London.

The show apartment of this development presents a dynamic, contemporary, and stylish interior design based on a warm color palette, rich materials, and smooth simple lines. Despite its limited square footage, an effective use of a few basic colors and simple furniture create a spacious living environment. A warm red wall distinguishes the living area from the adjacent dining area and all-white open-plan kitchen. The use of warm materials, such as leather and velvet, and rich colors, such as brown, black, and red, give an air of sophistication to this space.

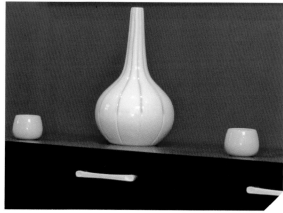

Surface: 807 sq ft

Location: London, United Kingdom

Completion date: March 2007

Photos: © Carlos Domínguez

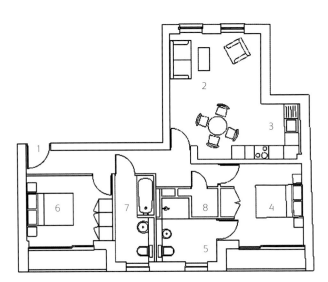

Floor plan

1. Entry
2. Living/dining room
3. Kitchen
4. Master bedroom
5. Master bathroom
6. Bedroom
7. Bathroom
8. Shower

A large leather-framed mirror in the bedroom is
a good way of creating the sensation of space
and luxury.

Clean simple lines and neutral colors create the perfect
soothing palette ready to be complemented with rich
colors and materials.

Sheer Elegance

Architect: Filippo Bombace

The renovation of this small apartment in the center of Rome—designed for a young professional woman—is dominated by contrasting volumes, created by a bold approximation of the kitchen to the shower—the centerpiece of this apartment. The open-plan layout is complemented by a meticulous color scheme, and the use of transparent materials and ambient lighting create a relaxed and sophisticated urban home.

Dark wengué flooring creates a visual continuity throughout the apartment and unites the individual domestic areas. A sheet of frosted glass separates a small entrance from the main living area, which consists of a corner sofa and a white console table by Dolmen. The dining area in the same space is defined by a bespoke dining table with a glass top. The table is symmetrically illuminated from below and above by spotlights fitted in the floor and ceiling. The shower-cum-fountain—the so-called *cubo doccia*—is the highlight of this apartment. Made of a base of Lecce stone, it is filled with river pebbles which are bathed in light and water, creating an interesting decorative feature as well as an interesting bathing experience.

Surface: 861 sq ft

Location: Rome, Italy

Completion date: 2005

Photos: © Luigi Filetici

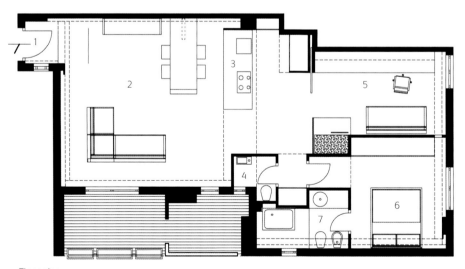

Floor plan

1. Entry
2. Living/dining room
3. Kitchen
4. Shower
5. Study
6. Bedroom
7. Bathroom

Illumination is an important feature in the interior design of this apartment. Halogen lights alternated with fluorescent tracker lights and soft colors make for a unique and sophisticated environment.

Futuristic Flair

Architect: Ajax Law Ling Kit, Virginia Lung

The basic idea behind this relatively small apartment in the capital of the Sichuan province is "wrapping." The apartment is defined by streamlined curves which integrate various domestic areas. A dark curved structure at the end of the main living space forms the sofa on one end and dining table on the other, while a similar white wrapping element forms the bed and wardrobe in the child's room. These structures hide the split-type air conditioner in the ceiling.

White is the primary color used throughout the apartment—white marble flooring, white walls, white beds, and white wardrobes—and is complemented by dark blue details. A large mirror in the living and dining room creates a double effect, making the place look bigger. It also reinforces the futuristic feel already created in this area by the curved structure. Mirrors are also used to the same effect in the master bedroom, which is defined by a round white futuristic-looking bed. A fluffy carpet adds some color to this minimal boudoir. The combination of a limited color scheme and rounded edges makes for a simple yet cozy urban family home.

Surface: 915 sq ft

Location: Chengdu, China

Completion date: 2007

Photos: © Gabriel Leung

Floor plan

1. Dining room
2. Living room
3. Kitchen
4. Balcony
5. Master bedroom
6. Children's room
7. Bathroom

A mirrored wardrobe is ideal in a small room as the limited space is literally doubled.

A room of contrasts: a shiny white rounded structure forms the bed and stands out on the fluffy dark-colored carpet and wall.

A tiled bathroom is the ultimate in luxury bathing.

Theatrical Antics

Architect: Ministry of Design

Originally a three-bedroom apartment, this home for a young urbanite couple is now a smart one-bedroom residence in the heart of metropolitan Singapore also incorporating a powder room, kitchen, living room, dining area, and two study nooks. The project reflects a desire to counter the sprawling city outside by creating a series of intimate tactile interior spaces.

The application of theatrical lighting and ceremonial transitions dramatizes the everyday rituals of sleeping, resting, eating, and cleansing, heightening the sensation of each. With a palette of warm colors and rich earthy textures, the interior creates a cocoon for the occupants of this home, an inner sanctum from the chaotic world outside. Floors, walls, and ceilings are covered in concrete and complemented by suede sofas, leather chairs, and soft fabric curtains and rugs. The space can be merged into one or separated into distinct areas depending on mood or needs, thanks to diaphanous fabric walls and raised walkways.

Surface: 915 sq ft

Location: Singapore City, Singapore

Completion date: september 2002

Photos: © Simon Devitt

Original floor plan

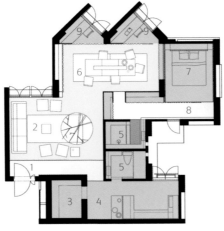

Current floor plan

1. Entry
2. Living room
3. Pantry
4. Kitchen
5. Bathroom
6. Dining room
7. Bedroom
8. Closet
9. Study

Tight Squeeze

Architect: NAP Architects

The goal was to build a home for a family of four—two parents and two children—in a densely built residential area of Tokyo. Disposing of a 430.5-square-foot site surrounded by buildings and only open to the north-facing side of the street, the architects had to come up with solutions for the lack of natural light and limited living space.

As walls are always on view in a house and even more so in a small one, Hiroshi Nakamura decided to transform one of the walls, creating different functions, dimensions, and expression in an extremely simple way. The street-facing wall was pushed out as far as possible, to the maximum building coverage, in order to enlarge the living room on the first floor. The result on the outside is a bump, while inside a curious soft hollow is shaped within. The wall becomes part of the inhabitants' lives—used as a comfortable bench to sit or lie on—and is an important feature of the house as a whole. Sunlight flowing down from the huge skylight at the top of the house is caught in this pouch and gently reflected to the rest of the room, providing different expressions of light on each floor. The structure also provides a sense of unity to this tiny house divided over several floors.

Surface: 936 sq ft

Location: Tokyo, Japan

Completion date: november 2005

Photos: © Daici Ano

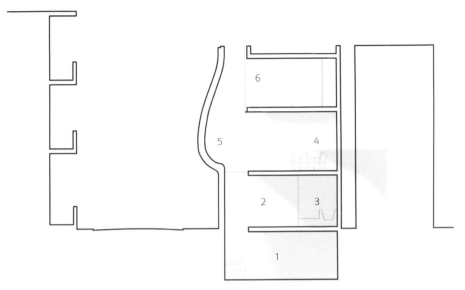

North-south section

1. Bedroom
2. Entry
3. Bathroom
4. Living/dining room
5. Light well
6. Children's room

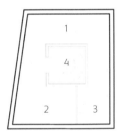

Basement

1. Reading room
2. Master bedroom
3. Closet
4. Light well

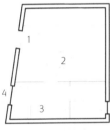

First floor

1. Entry
2. Light well
3. Bathroom
4. Bicycle parking

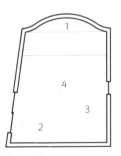

Second floor

1. Living room
2. Dining room
3. Kitchen
4. Light well

Third floor

1. Child's room
2. Child's room
3. Light well

Floor plans

The soft hollow in the north-facing wall is an interesting feature of this small house and provides a sense of structure to the whole.

The pouch catches light coming down from the skylight and distributes it to the rest of the home.

A skylight at the top of the house solves the problem of lack of light in a densely built urban area.

Smallish

Central Comfort

Architect: YLAB

A former office space, this penthouse in Barcelona's most emblematic square, Plaza Cataluña, is the weekend home of an English couple who wanted an apartment with all the services and comfort of a top-class hotel. The brief required a functional design with plenty of storage, preferably hidden, and an extremely comfortable and sophisticated space including all technological advances in terms of security, automation, audio, video, and climatization.

Considering the small and long floor plan oriented towards the terrace, it was important to mark the space's most extreme limits and allow a visual program to develop the length of the space by removing partition walls and replacing them with movable elements. The limits— floor, exterior wall, and ceiling—were underlined by an ivory cream color contrasted by one piece of furniture in dark gray elm wood running the length of the space from the kitchen to the bedroom. This piece of furniture separates the private from the public areas and incorporates all of the home's functional and technical requirements. It successfully defines spaces, while at the same time creating order in each different area, incorporating kitchenware at one end and a wardrobe and the built-in television in the bathroom at the other.

Surface: 969 sq ft

Location: Barcelona, Spain

Completion date: 2006

Photos: © Stephan Zaehring

In order to create a spacious and flowing interior, partition walls were removed and replaced with movable elements.

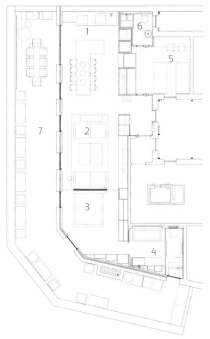

Floor plan

1. Kitchen/dining room
2. Living room
3. Master bedroom
4. Master bathroom
5. Children's room
6. Bathroom
7. Terrace

The kitchen is made of extra-wide modules with
handle-free surfaces made of a bronze-colored
aluminum and polished sandstone worktops.

The kitchen is the focal point of the house. This
meeting area is defined by a three-dimensional play
of protruding elements.

A large piece of furniture that runs the length of the apartment hides kitchen utensils and electrical appliances, including the oven, dishwasher, and refrigerataor.

Small hidden cupboards, which can be opened by
applying pressure to the doors, are incorporated into
the bathroom walls.

Maximum Compliance

Architects: Gary Chang, Raymond Chan

Essentially a three-bedroom unit, the inhabitants of this apartment interact with the space and can create a different combination of spaces in order to give them more freedom in domestic living, allowing normal and unexpected activities to unfold. In response to the single-child policy in China, the brief requested that the extra bedroom be transformed into a study.

To provide flexibility to the overall layout of the apartment and "liberate" the extra room from its assigned purpose, the architects decided to create a relationship between this room and the others. A pivoting wall cabinet is the centerpiece of the apartment, key element of the living room, and envelope of the study. The cabinet can be flipped, combined, or separated to create numerous different areas. When flipped open, the study fuses with the living area and reveals a large fluid space. An aisle links the living area to the master bedroom through the study. This area can be partially opened or open on three sides. When totally open, half of the apartment becomes entirely barrier-free. By shutting off the elements in the living area, a separate living unit is formed for the couple and when all the movable pieces are closed, the apartment returns to a typical three-room unit.

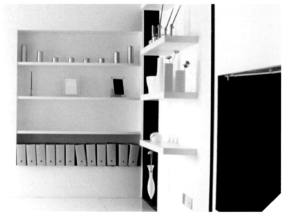

Surface: 969 sq ft

Location: Guangzhou, China

Completion date: 2005

Photos: © EDGE Design Institute

A pivoted wall cabinet allows the spaces of this
apartment to interact and a number of different areas
are created.

When totally open, the study and living room fuse and
half the apartment becomes totally barrier-free.

To provide more flexibility in the overall layout of the apartment, the study can be closed off or integrated with the living room as required.

Literary Heights

Architect: Juan Antonio Gómez González

This duplex is one of six apartments in La Casa de les Lletres, where each unit is inspired and named after a Catalan poet or writer and has a unique avant-garde design that blends with a century-old tradition and literary ambience.

This luxury space enjoys a huge double-height dining/living room, a fully equipped kitchen, two bathrooms, and two double bedrooms. A mix of materials and colors creates a cozy and urban environment, while literature leaves its mark on the architecture. Hardwood floors absorb the abundant light that comes in through the old renovated windows. This light, in turn, bounces off the glass panel—stamped with extracts of the Catalan writer's prose—which makes up the corten steel staircase. The upstairs rooms are completely independent from the main living space downstairs, though the design is consistent throughout.

Surface: 969 sq ft

Location: Barcelona, Spain

Completion date: 2001

Photos: © Gogortza / Llorella

Josep Pla
El quadern gris
1965

ue em donarà els diners
...ixit i còmode i per a comprar
...t grossa, de cuiro autèntic,
... les maletes petites no tenen
...ests viatges"

Josep Pla
El quadern gris
1965

Floor plan

1. Entry
2. Kitchen
3. Living/dining room
4. Stairs
5. Bedroom
6. Bathroom

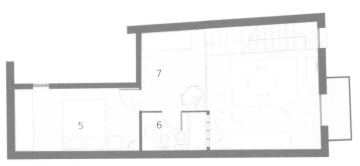

Mezzanine

7. Living room

A combination of warm colors and materials creates
a cozy living environment.

Dainty Distinction

Architect: Alan Barr, Bree Dahl

A young professional couple living in New York City wanted a relaxing, comfortable, and clutter-free space to return to after a heavy workday or long business trip. Situated in a prewar building in Brooklyn with 9.8-foot-high ceilings and many of the original moldings and details intact, the space already had plenty of character. The space was kept clean and neutral with off-white walls. The existing architecture was embraced and complemented with special antique lighting fixtures, an eclectic furniture collection, and artwork and accessories collected on the couple's travels.

Both professionals in the architecture and interior design industry, the owners of this urban residence have eclectic and individual tastes, which is reflected in their home where they combine one-off antiques with Moroccan kilims and store-bought pieces. The south wall of the dining room stands out as a centerpiece covered with black and white paisley Cole & Son wallpaper. A work in progress, the owners are always on the lookout for that next great piece to incorporate into the fabric of their lives.

Surface: 990 sq ft

Location: New York, NY, USA

Completion date: April 2006

Photos: © Eric Laignel

The owners love salvaging architectural artifacts and
antiques, restoring unique pieces, and incorporating
them into their lives.

Clean, neutral, off-white walls are the perfect
background to offset the eclectic collection
of furniture, artwork, and accessories in this
young professional couple's home.

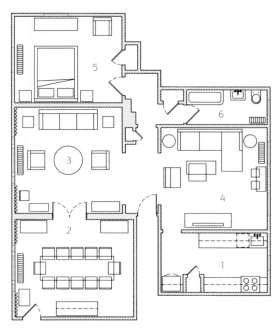

Floor plan

1. Kitchen
2. Dining room
3. Sitting area
4. Living room
5. Bedroom
6. Bathroom

The white console piece in the dining room was found
in an antique store in Brooklyn. It was stripped,
painted white, then a new mirrored back piece
and a stone top were added.

Dark stained floors were chosen to hide the existing
blonde wood parquet and add a sense of drama
to the space.

The master bed was custom designed by the
owners and produced by Mueller Custom Cabinetry
in California.

Antique light fixtures were sourced from all over the
United States and vary in style from midcentury to art
deco. Many are former schoolhouse light fixtures.

Blossoming Interior

Architect: Ippolito Fleitz Group

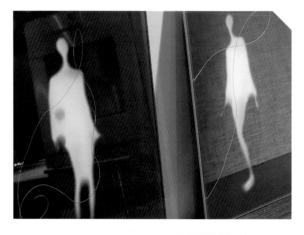

This atelier apartment is situated in an exclusive apartment complex in one of Stuttgart's prime residential areas and is the client's new base for both her professional and private life. The brief was to create an emotional, personal, and feminine living space as well as a clear and focused working environment in a relatively small area.

Located on the third floor and bordered by a long strip of windows on one side, the apartment enjoys plenty of natural light. The layout of the apartment is essentially an elongated rectangle with two long hallways running along either side. It is divided into clear zones creating the required private, semipublic, and common areas. With clear-cut cubic forms and the uniform materiality of smoked oak floors and furnishings, the interior designers established the basis for a calm and uncluttered spatial impression, while the use of colors and textiles in different areas set extra atmospheric accents for each space. The bathroom by the entrance, for example, is covered in a textile that conveys both depth and softness. A cozy upholstered seating area with floor-to-ceiling velvet velour-covered, diamond-stitched side panels fills a niche in the corner of the dining and work space and adds a touch of sophistication. A field of flowers designed by Monica Trenkler and decorating the ceiling connects all areas of the apartment and also adds a feminine touch.

Surface: 1,012 sq ft

Location: Stuttgart, Germany

Completion date: 2007

Photos: © Zooey Braun

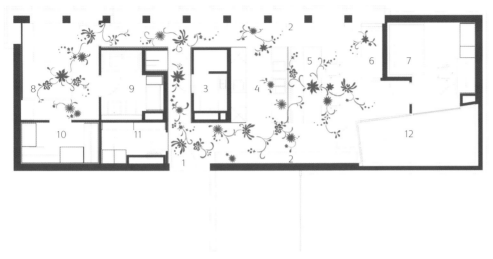

Floor plan

1. Entry
2. Hallway
3. Bathroom
4. Kitchen
5. Dining room/office
6. Living room
7. Guest room
8. Master bedroom
9. Master bathroom
10. Dressing room
11. Mirrored closet
12. Balcony

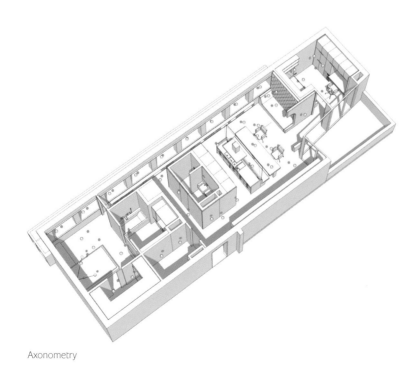

Axonometry

A clear sheet of glass separates the kitchen from the dining and work space, which is defined by a long upholstered bench attached to the back of the freestanding kitchen.

The space beneath the bench contributes to the dual function of the dining/work space: two retractable elements at foot level hide a printer, scanner, and enough storage space for additional work materials.

The kitchen is at the center of the apartment—a nod to the client's character (she is a keen cook). This space is made up of contrasting materials: a concrete countertop and wooden cabinets.

White leather chesterfield upholstery surrounding three sides of the bed turns this room into an opulent guest room, which also serves as a small study, with a desk incorporated into a wall unit.

A mirrored wall to the left of the entrance multiplies the view of one of the corridors ad infinitum.

The bedroom has an en suite bathroom and an adjacent dressing room. The solid surface of the bathroom walls are engraved with specially chosen quotations.

One wall of the bedroom is painted in mauve and the headboard is covered in the same velvet velour covering the seating niche in the main living space.

LASS DIE GROSSEN ELEMENTE
DIESEN ANBRECHENDEN TAG SEGNEN:

DIE ERDE MIT IHREM DUFT,
DAS WASSER MIT SEINEM GESCHMACK,
DAS FEUER MIT SEINEM LEUCHTEN,
DIE LUFT MIT IHRER BERÜHRUNG
UND DER RAUM MIT SEINEN TÖNEN.

Gracefully Chic

Architect: Jordi Queralt

Once a compartmentalized three-bedroom apartment, the space of this Mediterranean home was maximized by knocking down partition walls and relocating the kitchen. To provide continuity within the home, the same materials and colors were used in all the rooms. The architects chose three main colors: brown, black, and white. Wengué wood is used for the floor and also for the bespoke coffee table in the living room, and the bed frame and night tables in the bedroom. White was chosen for the color of the walls, kitchen furniture, dining chairs and table, the bookcase, and guest bathroom, while black is the dominant color of the master bathroom, the wardrobe, and the television and reading area. The lighting is specific to each space, creating a particular ambience as and when needed.

The use of color and light to define domestic areas is very effective in an open-plan space. The kitchen is clearly a separate entity, though the universal wood floor and the long dining table connect it with the adjacent living area. The use of white and black makes the cooking and dining area a very neutral room but with plenty of personality. In addition, smooth surfaces help maintain a clutter-free space. A perfect example of this is the ingenious space solution for an office space in the living room. The interior of a decorative chimney serves as a cupboard for office materials, hidden behind the front of the chimney is a sliding door suspended from the ceiling.

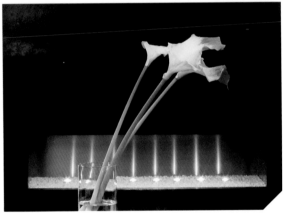

Surface: 1022 sq ft

Location: Barcelona, Spain

Completion date: 2005

Photos: © Jordi Miralles

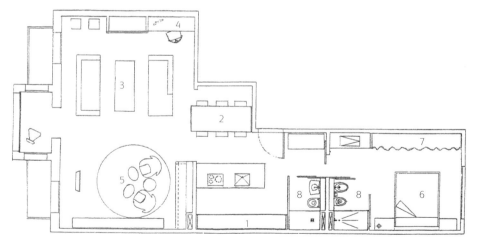

Floor plan

1. Kitchen
2. Dining room
3. Living room
4. Office
5. Reading/
   television area
6. Bedroom
7. Closet
8. Bathroom

The use of three neutral colors—white, black, and brown—gives this urban home a very sophisticated feel, complemented by atmospheric lighting in each separate space.

Smooth surfaces help maintain a clutter-free kitchen, while the neutral colors accentuate the overall style of this designer kitchen, which includes products by Miele and Bang & Olufsen, among others.

A black velvet curtain hides the contents of the wall-
to-wall wardrobe, as reflected in the mirror behind the
bed, which gives the room depth and luminosity.

A low bed with night tables as an extension of the bed frame made of wengué wood give the impression of little volume, despite the king size bed.

Tangerine Space

Architect: Entre4parets

The main idea behind the renovation of this 1,055-square-foot apartment in Barcelona was to renovate the interior and make open spaces the most important feature. Complemented with colors that exude personality, comfort, and originality, the apartment's largest open space is dedicated to the main living and dining area, measuring 326 square feet.

With the use of warm colors and transparent materials throughout, the architects have created a comfortable and elegant urban interior. The core of the home is the living and dining area which is defined by natural Cumarú flooring, an orange wall of glass—of the adjacent small bathroom—and a large red sofa in the living room. A personal touch is added to the long, narrow kitchen cabinets with high-pressure, decorative, laminated images exclusively designed by Entre4parets. The use of transparent blinds at the end of this space makes this a bright cooking area.

Surface: 1,055 sq ft

Location: Barcelona, Spain

Completion date: February 2007

Photos: © Sandra Pereznieto

A hallway leads to a large open space which incorporates the main living and dining area characterized by its warm tones of red and orange.

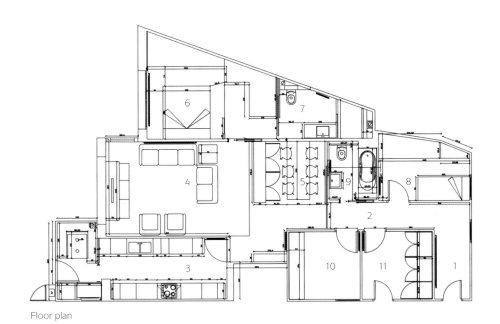

Floor plan

1. Entry
2. Hallway
3. Kitchen
4. Living room
5. Dining room
6. Master bedroom
7. Master bathroom
8. Children's room
9. Bathroom
10. Library
11. Laundry room

Simple straight lines and neutral colors create a
clutter-free area perfect for nighttime rest.

Depth is created in a small, brightly tiled bathroom by
covering one wall with a large mirror.

Contemporary Beginnings

Architect: Filippo Bombace

The first home of a young couple, this small attic in Rome contains a valuable family legacy. So as not to overbear the place—already filled with family heirlooms—the architects chose a neutral, clear, and severe interior. The house is defined by a limited use of materials—wengué wood flooring and statutory marble in the bathroom—and the only elements breaking up the "silence" of the austere color scheme are the big red sofa—*Globe* by Moroso—and *Cuore*, the light installation by Czech artist Svetlana Kuliskova. The traditional dining room is integrated into the spacious kitchen to let the common areas breathe.

The hallway leading to the bedroom is like a walk-through closet, with plenty of cupboard space on one side of the hall. The master bedroom with a Poliform bed and wardrobe includes an en suite bathroom separated by a large sliding panel. A small window in the wall, which separates the bathroom from the sleeping area, puts the wood shower pan on display, while a glossy glass opening in the bathroom offers a window of additional natural light to the living room. The only decorative elements in the marble bathroom are modern Zucchetti faucets. The small elements of steel reflect the light in this space and add a touch of elegance.

Surface: 1,076 sq ft

Location: Rome, Itlay

Completion date: 2007

Photos: © Luigi Filetici

Floor plan

1. Entry
2. Living room
3. Kitchen
4. Hallway with closets
5. Master bedroom
6. Master bathroom
7. Guest room
8. Guest bathroom
9. Terrace

A Poliform built-in wardrobe with smooth lines integrates into the simple bedroom and is reflected in the wengué wood floors.

The wood shower pan can be seen through a small window in the wall separating the bathroom from the bedroom.

Inner Peace

Architect: UdA

This apartment located in a 1960s building in the center of Turin was completely renovated to make it a bright and spacious home. Every element of this urban home was carefully contemplated and furniture was designed to transcend everyday reality.

The original parquet and resin flooring was painted black and vertical partitions in extra-clear glass were inserted. The interior designer played with contrasts—white and black, day and night, natural and artificial. Light bounces off the white ceiling and walls, which also enhances the spread of light throughout, while the dark is absorbed by the black-tinted floorboards. An Asian inspiration can be found in the precise and accurate, yet simple, composition and details of the elements, such as the bespoke furniture which does not intrude in the overall layout of the space. Rather, every piece of furniture is cohesive and plays an important role in this contemplative space.

Surface: 1,076 sq ft

Location: Turin, Italy

Completion date: 2006

Photos: © Grazia Branco/Ike Branco Productions

Floor plan

1. Entry
2. Kitchen
3. Dining room
4. Living room
5. Laundry room
6. Closet
7. Bedroom
8. Bathroom
9. Bathroom

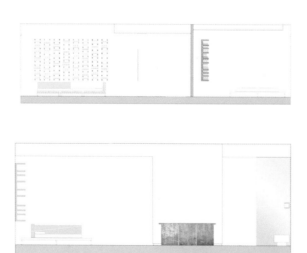

Section

The furniture was specially made so that it plays an important role in the apartment without interfering with the layout.

Inspired by the spirit of the Japanese art of ikebana, the composition of the elements is precise and accurate, yet simple.

Every element in this apartment has a deliberate quality of lightness, punctuated every so often with thought-provoking pieces, to create an urban haven for contemplation.

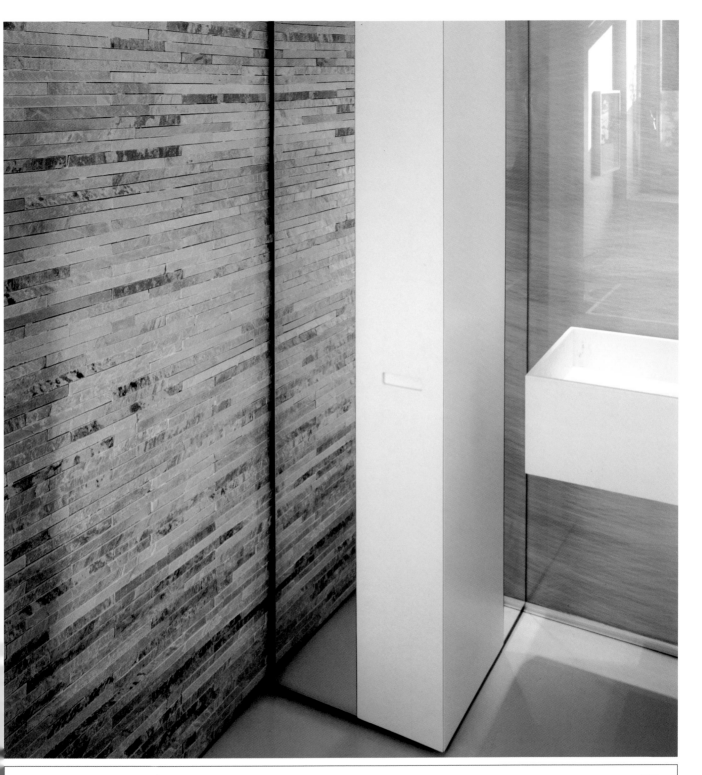

Sweet Transformation

Architect: David Hicks

Designed for the architect himself, this apartment is located in a former chocolate factory, Red Tulip, which is now an apartment building in a progressive part of inner city Melbourne. A ten-square L-shaped footprint, the design of this apartment was a study of the personal environment and rationalization and justification of limited space. With only one facade of glazing facing south, the need to create a sense of light, as well as space, was paramount.

Taking into consideration scale, reflectivity in materials, and new ways of construction, the space was transformed into a luxurious quality home. The architect managed to minimize the environment to achieve a maximization of space. Despite its limited dimensions, the apartment's 10.5-foot slab-to-slab height offers many possibilities. A raised platform was incorporated to allow flexibility with the services. This black gloss platform containing the kitchen and dining area provides a notional division between this space and the lounge. The kitchen was restricted to a 15.5-foot-long area, with all appliances concealed within a streamlined cantilevered credenza unit. A further segmenting of the space is created by the use of a grid formula based on the existing white terrazzo Romastone floor tiles. By placing certain elements within the grid, a precise and rational environment is created, accentuating the order, color scheme, furnishings, and materials.

Surface: 1,076 sq ft

Location: Melbourne, Australia

Completion date: 2002

Photos: © Trevor Mein

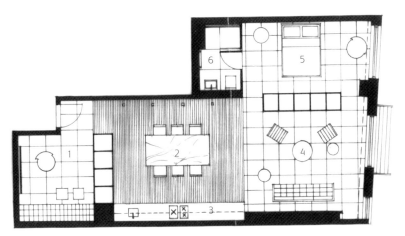

Floor plan

1. Entrance hall
2. Dining room
3. Kitchen
4. Lounge
5. Bedroom
6. Bathroom

A seamless joinery unit placed within the grids on the floor separates the more private sleeping and bathing area from the public space.

The scaling up of materials, reflectivity, and choice of seamless products along with strong planning and utilization of space combine to create a minimal space with a maximized effect.

All materials were incorporated as large panels, as seen in the bathroom, where the use of silver cladding seamlessly lines the space.

Fashionable Intervention

Architects: Greg Natale, Stacey Pappas

Cove Apartments, designed by Harry Seidler, in Sydney's The Rocks district, is the city's fourth tallest residential tower. With a combination of sumptuous finishes—such as ebony veneer, Gregio Carico marble, Persian carpets, polished materials, and paint finishes—the somber glossy interior of this apartment is a reflection of the clever use of luxurious materials in this landmark building.

The main living area is bordered on one end by huge floor-to-ceiling windows offering spectacular views over the city and by large mirrors on the other creating an expansive effect. The overall darkness of this space—the dark timber of the cantilevered credenza and the charcoal grays of the floor and kitchen—is juxtaposed by bright accents of colorful Missoni floral prints. The general dark color is further broken up by geometric Missoni prints used on traditional silhouettes adding visual interest. Similarly, a dramatic effect is created in the bedroom with a traditional decorative headboard and bold Missoni zig-zag quilt.

Surface: 1,076 sq ft

Location: Sydney, Australia

Completion date: November 2006

Photos: © Sharrin Rees

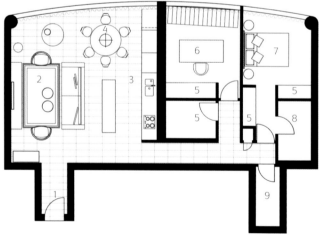

Floor plan

1. Entry
2. Living room
3. Kitchen
4. Dining room
5. Closet
6. Guest room/study
7. Master bedroom
8. En suite bathroom
9. Laundry room

Floor-to-ceiling windows not only offer spectacular
views over Sydney but also reflect the space, creating
an illusion of expanse in this apartment.

The darkness of this apartment is broken up by
geometric Missoni prints on the upholstery.

A gold-colored baroque headboard and bold Missoni
zig-zag quilt stand out in the darkness of this opulent
master bedroom.

Brighter colors were chosen for the study/guest room,
though the velvet materials are still in keeping with the
ambience created in the rest of the apartment.

Cool Passion

Architect: Antony Chan

A mix of fiery red and cool white, passion in the midst of a calming haven, this Hong Kong apartment blends the mood of the 1970s with today's contemporary styles to create a dramatic yet comfortable urban living environment.

A stunning living area is created by the contrast of energetic red colors on a soothing white background. A mirrored glass wall decorated with round red shapes is the centerpiece of the living room. The combination of passionate red and peaceful white is applied throughout this residence to create an exciting and dynamic, yet clean and consistent interior design. This duotone color scheme is complemented by the use of transparent materials to help create a sensation of space and lightness and a mix of retro and contemporary furniture. For example, a mirrored corridor is spruced up with touches of red and household appliances and various decorative elements are in tones of red and white.

Surface: 1,100 sq ft

Location: Hong Kong, China

Completion date: 2007

Photos: © Virgile Simon Bertrand

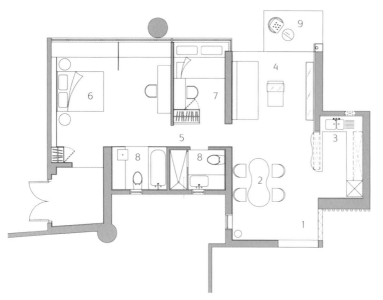

Floor plan

1. Entry
2. Dining room
3. Kitchen
4. Living room
5. Hallway
6. Master bedroom
7. Bedroom
8. Bathroom
9. Balcony

A backlit wall made of a clear glass panel decorated with round red shapes gives a dramatic edge to the master bedroom.

Domestic Bliss

Architect: DAP Studio

Situated on the fourteenth floor of a residential building in the heart of Milan, this apartment enjoys wonderful panoramic views of the city and receives plenty of daylight. Elena Sacco and Paolo Danelli—the designers—consider this a "place of well-being," where the individual is at the center of the home, not the domestic tasks that need to be carried out. Thus, within the domestic environment, the different functions become an integral part of the system of the house. The main aim of this project was to create a fluid open-plan space without closing off or blocking out any views.

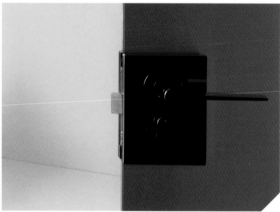

The traditional subdivision of the day and night zones is not clear in this apartment. Organized in an open plan, the space continues, gradually becoming more private and finally closing around the sleeping area. The gradualness of this process allows a series of intermediate spaces to be individualized and at the same time creates different degrees of transparency. The organization of the space essentially revolves around the furniture and dividing elements. The day area is defined by a semiopen kitchen, which can be closed off by a glass screen, on which images can also be projected. The day area is separated from the night area by other transparent dividing elements. A harmonious ambience is created throughout by the use of soft colors and lighting, while the use of transparent and reflective materials help maintain a strong visual fluidity throughout the apartment.

Surface: 1,205 sq ft

Location: Milan, Italy

Completion date: 2005

Photos: © Andrea Martiradonna

The main objective of this apartment in the heart of
Milan was to create a fluid open-plan space allowing
the different areas to flow into each other.

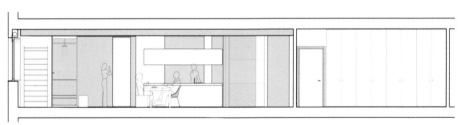

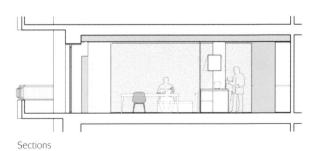

Sections

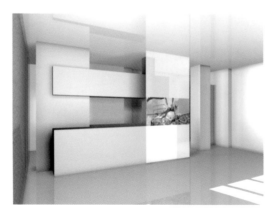

Rendering

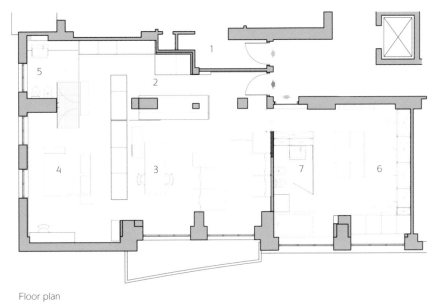

Floor plan

1. Entry
2. Kitchen
3. Living/dining room
4. Master bedroom
5. Master bathroom
6. Guest room
7. Guest bathroom

Maximal Minimalism

Architect: CUBO Design Architect

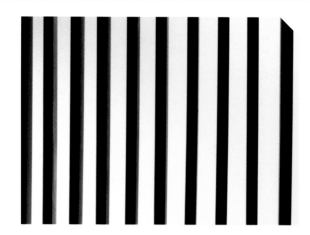

This project was built in an urban residential district within the Nagano Prefecure in central Japan, on land that was originally a parking lot. In cooperation with the client, the architect managed to address the unique challenges of the site and create an efficient and comfortable home insulated against the severe cold of Nagano winters.

The exterior of the house is formed minimally with angled walls which provide graceful slopes upward toward the roofline. Inside, the walnut floors and white walls provide a wonderfully elegant contrast. The living room on the second floor also serves as a guest room and is set up with a *tatami* space. The use of Japanese-style lattice creates a division between the different areas while allowing continuity at the same time so that family members can sense the presence of others in nearby rooms. True to the traditional Japanese interior design style of Zen, the house is filled with only necessary furniture and is void of decoration—letting the hardwood floors, lattice, and white walls create the desired effect.

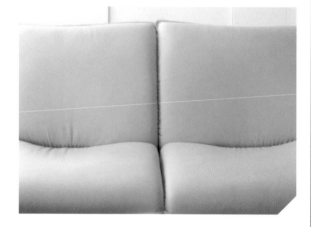

Surface: 1,248 sq ft

Location: Matsumoto City, Japan

Completion date: March 2005

Photos: © Yasuno Sakata

First floor

Floor plans

1. Bedroom
2. Bathroom
3. Bathroom
4. Kitchen
5. Living room
6. Dining room

Second floor

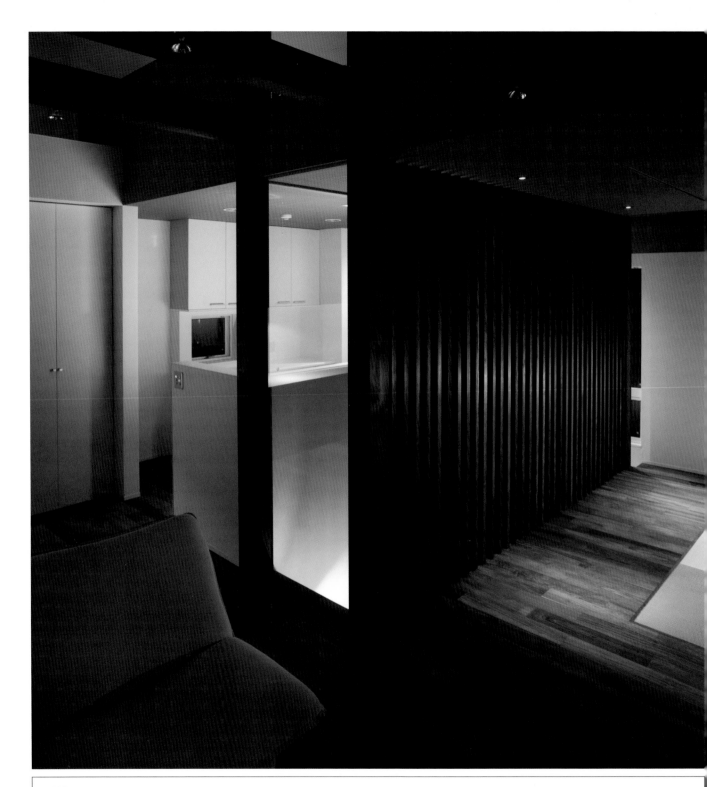

A lattice structure on the second floor is the only
decorative element and serves to divide the spaces
while still allowing continuity between them.

Center Stage

Architects: J. L. de Madariaga, Mluz Martínez

The main objective of this apartment in the center of Valladolid—a city in the northeast of the Iberian Peninsula—was to create a fresh, open, and contemporary home where spaces, illumination, and furniture become parts of a whole. The property's structural elements as well as the holes in the existing facade were maintained and incorporated into the new distribution of space, which included two bedrooms, a bathroom, kitchen with access to a back patio, a living/dining area, and entrance hall.

The interior design is based on open spaces, good materials, a careful study of illumination and color scheme, and a scarce yet rigorous selection of furniture. As the apartment is located on the mezzanine level between the ground and first floors, there is not much natural light. Despite this, the architect dared to use dark gray-black colors for the main living area. The effect is mitigated by specific lighting used throughout the home.

Surface: 1,259 sq ft

Location: Valladolid, Spain

Completion date: 2006

Photos: © Jordi Miralles

The entrance hall flows into the open dining and
living area, creating a large open space for relaxing
and entertaining.

Because this apartment lacks a generous income of
natural light, the architects used specific lighting
throughout to create a special atmosphere.

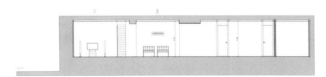

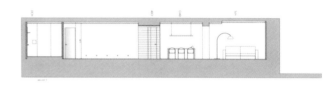

Sections

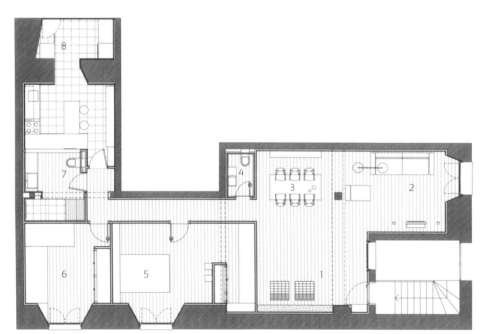

Floor plan

1. Entry
2. Living room
3. Dining room
4. Bathroom
5. Master bedroom
6. Children's room
7. Bathroom
8. Kitchen

In contrast to the dark colors used in the living room, the bedroom is completely white, which creates a calming environment.

ducha

Squared Angle

Architect: Saaj Design

This small house in St. Kilda—a bayside suburb of Melbourne and the Victorian capital's favorite playground—required varying and multiple spaces within a limited building area. The house is oriented toward the rear facing public parkland, and its surrounding urban condition is dominated by Edwardian roofs, terra-cotta tiles, and brick chimneys.

The building rotates off the orthogonal axis of the side boundaries to address the rear, angled, boundary. This transition is marked by glass-framed vertical "tears." A double-story, steel-framed glass window is a maquette of the overall form, folding in the opposite plane. It is divided at the crease and the lower panel can be opened to allow the main living space to open out onto the rear garden. The vertical nature of the space is celebrated within with a mezzanine setting off two adjacent walls. The sense of space is further accentuated by the use of transparent materials and limited furniture and decoration. Mood lighting, the exposed beams, and dark brown floorboards offset the white walls, giving this minimal open space a cozy and stylish feel.

Surface: 1,388 sq ft

Location: Melbourne, Australia

Completion date: 2006

Photos: © Patrick Redmond

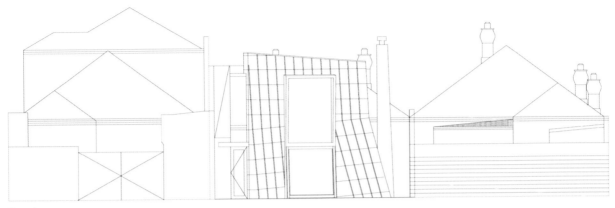

Elevation

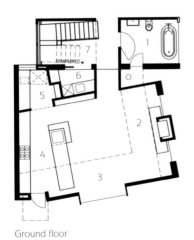

Ground floor

Floor plan

1. Bathroom
2. Living room
3. Dining room
4. Kitchen
5. Pantry
6. Laundry room
7. Stairs
8. Bedroom/study
9. Living room

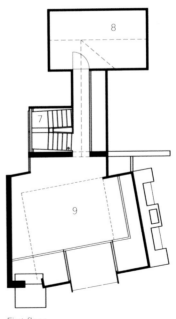

First floor

The clean straight lines and clear colors used
throughout create relaxing and sophisticated interiors.

Despite a sparse use of furniture, a second, more
intimate living area is created on the mezzanine level.

A mirror that runs along one side of the room makes this bathroom look twice its size.

Directory

208 Ajax Law Ling Kit & Virginia Lung
One Plus Partnership
4/F, 332 Lockhart Road
Wanchai, Hong Kong
China
T. +852 2591 9308
F. +852 2591 9362
admin@onepluspartnership.com
www.onepluspartnership.com

214 Mohen Design International
No.18, Alley 396, Wulumuqi S. Road
200031 Shanghai
China
T. +862 1643 709 010
mohen@mohen-design.com
www.mohen-design.com

222 New ID Interiors
Unit 9, Capitol Park
Capitol Way
London NW9 0EQ
UK
T. +44 208 200 5556
F. +44 208 200 1455
interiors@new-id.co.uk
www.new-id.co.uk

230 Filippo Bombace
Via Monte Tomatico 1
00141 Rome
Italy
T. +39 6 868 98266
F. +39 6 868 98529
info@filippobombaccom
www.filippobombaccom

240 Ajax Law Ling Kit & Virginia Lung
One Plus Partnership
4/F, 332 Lockhart Road
Wanchai, Hong Kong
China
T. +852 2591 9308
F. +852 2591 9362
admin@onepluspartnership.com
www.onepluspartnership.com

248 Ministry of Design
16B Trengganu Street
058470 Singapore
T. +65 6222 5780
F. +65 6222 5781
studio@modonlincom
www.modonlincom

254 Hiroshi Nakamura
NAP Architects
Sky Heights 3-1-9-5F
Tamagawa Setagaya-ku
158-0094 Tokyo
Japan
T. +81 3 3709 7936
F. +81 3 3709 7963
nakamura@nakam.info
www.nakam.info

266 YLAB
Pallars 85-91 4° 6ª
08018 Barcelona
Spain
T. +34 934 864 807
F. +37 934 864 808
info@ylab.es
www.ylab.es

276 Gary Chang, Raymond Chan
EDGE Design Institute
Suite 1604, Eastern Harbour Centre
28 Hoi Chak Street
Quarry Bay, Hong Kong
China
T. + 852 2802 6212
F. + 852 2802 6213
edgeltd@netvigator.com
www.edgedesign.com.hk

286 Juan Antonio Gómez González
Av. Generalitat, 36
08754 El Papiol (Barcelona)
Spain
T. +34 936 731 686
F. +34 936 730 725
jagomez@grupcru.com
www.grupcru.com

294 Alan Barr, Bree Dahl
Zeff Design
515 West 20th Street, 4W
NY, NY 10011
USA
T. +1 212 580 7090
F. +1 212 580 7181
abarr@zeffdesign.com
www.zeffdesign.com

304 Ippolito Fleitz Group
Bismarckstrasse 67 B
70197 Stuttgart
Germany
T. +49 711 993392 330
F. + 49 711 993392 333
info@ifgroup.org
www.ifgroup.org

318 Jordi Queralt
T. +34 666 922 525

328 Entre4parets
Berguedà, 7
08028 Barcelona
Spain
T. +34 934 191 333
F. +34 934 103 894
disseny@entre4parets.com
www.entre4parets.com

336 Filippo Bombace
Via Monte Tomatico 1
00141 Rome
Italy
T. +39 6 868 98266
F. +39 6 868 98529
info@filippobombaccom
www.filippobombaccom

346 UdA
Via Valprato, 68
10155 Turin
Italy
T. +39 1 124 89489
F. +39 1 124 87591
uda@uda.it
www.uda.it

358 David Hicks
PO Box 6110 Chapel Street North
South Yarra Victoria 3141
Australia
T. +61 3 9826 3955
F. +61 3 9826 3988
david@davidhicks.com.au
www.davidhicks.com.au

366 Greg Natale, Stacey Pappas
Studio 6, Level 3
35 Buckingham Street
Surry Hills NSW 2010
Australia
T. +61 2 8399 2103
F. +61 2 8399 3104
info@gregnatalcom
www.gregnatalcom

376 Antony Chan
10/F, 88 Hing Fat Street
Hong Kong
China
T. +852 2147 1297
F. +852 2147 0118
info@cream.com.hk
www.cream.com.hk

384 DAP Studio
Via G. B. Brocchi, 7/a
20131 Milan
Italy
T. + 39 2 706 31511
F. + 39 2 236 1496
dap@newsmedia.it
www.dapstudio.com

392 CUBO Design Architect
3-17-20, Hishinuma
Chigasaki City, Kanawaga
apan
T. +81 467 54 6994
F. +81 467 54 7035
cubo@cubod.com
www.cubod.com

400 J. L. de Madariaga, Mluz Martínez
San Ignacio, 9 portal 3 bajo
47003 Valladolid
Spain
T. + 34 649 959 697
F. + 34 98 337 2440
jldemadariaga@terra.es

412 Saaj Design
222 Bluff Road
Sandringham Victoria 3191
Australia
T. +61 3 9598 1996
F. +61 3 9598 1997
saaj@bigpond.net.au
ww.saaj.com.au